SEO for Beginners: Step-by-step beginners' guide to dominate the first page

Table of Contents

Disclaimer 5

Introduction 6

Getting Started With SEO 8

    What is SEO? 8

    Various Terms Related To Search Engine Optimization 9

Various Types of White Hat SEO Techniques 13

    On-Page SEO Techniques 13

        Top On-Page SEO Techniques for High Ranking 14

    Off-page SEO Techniques 31

        Off-page SEO Techniques for Impressing Google 33

Content Marketing & Social Media Marketing 40

    Content Marketing 41

    Social Media Marketing 43

Can you make a difference with just one type of marketing? 45

Everything that you need to know about Keywords 47

    Importance of Using Keywords & Keyword Research 47

    Keyword Research Tools for Finding New Keywords 49

        Google Keyword Planner Tool........................ 50

    Long Tail Keyword Pro 53

    Jaaxy 53

    SEMrush.. 54

    Keyword.io.. 55

    My Personal Recommendation........................ 56

Marketing with Google Adwords 57

    Why is it important to advertise your business?. 57

    How to set up a profitable ad using Google Adwords... 59

Conclusion 68

Disclaimer

Copyright © 2016

All Rights Reserved

No part of this book can be transmitted or reproduced in any form including print, electronic, photocopying, scanning, mechanical or recording without prior written permission from the author.

While the author has taken the utmost effort to ensure the accuracy of the written content, all readers are advised to follow information mentioned herein at their own risk. The author cannot be held responsible for any personal or commercial damage caused by information. All readers are encouraged to seek professional advice when needed.

Introduction

So, you've created an amazing-looking website which makes everyone say WOW! And you have even created a lot of content on it, which is free from grammatical mistakes and plagiarism. But what now?

Most people today give up on their online journey after some time because they do not see any results. No one visits their website and no conversation occurs on their written articles. This, in turn, demotivates them. Well, we all have been through that stage, I have been through that stage. But, instead of giving up, I looked for a solution. The solution for this problem is to start doing SEO on your website.

Now, you can either wait for nights and days for the angel to come and tell Google and other search engines about your website. Or, you can take responsibility and understand that no angel or tooth fairy will come to help you and **eventually you need to start working for yourself.**

If you are a dreamer, then I want you to stop reading this book right now as this book is for hard workers. And if you are one and want to work for yourself, then I really want to congratulate and welcome you. I have written this book solely for telling people more and more about SEO. Why? Because whenever I talk to someone and tell them to do some SEO, they eventually give up as SEO is a huge task and can be overwhelming. SEO is definitely a huge and a complex task, however, it does not mean that you cannot do it. With the help of this book, you will be able to do some high-quality SEO for your website. It does not matter what your skill level is in online marketing, this book will surely be of help to you as I have written this book keeping beginners in mind.

At the end of this book, you will not only understand what SEO is, but you will also know about various types of SEO techniques and how you can use Google Adwords to make your business a success. So, let's get started!

Getting Started With SEO

So, let's start fresh as this is the book for beginners. Let's first understand what the term SEO means.

What is SEO?

SEO stands for Search Engine Optimization and is also known as search engine optimizer among some online marketers. Search Engine Optimization is a step by step technique that is used by almost all online marketers to get high rankings in various search engines like Yahoo, Google, etc., so that they can get high traffic from these search engines to their website. Traffic refers to the people who were using Google or any other search engine to search for information on a topic.

Search engine optimization helps your website get noticed by people all over the world by improving its chances of being found by search engines.

For example, let's say that your website is about how to stop your dog from barking and it has an article on the same topic. So, when someone searches on

Google or Yahoo for "how to stop a dog from barking", the place of your website on the pages of the search results will be determined by how well your site is optimized for search engines. The better search engine optimization is done, the higher the place of your website link in the search engine pages will be. The poorer your search engine optimization is, the lower a place you will get.

I have seen people with average content rankings on-page one of Google, and some people with amazing content rankings on-page two or page three of Google search engine rankings. It is all because of the SEO techniques being used by the site admins.

Now, that said, let's move on and learn some of the terms that beginners come across over the internet when getting started with search engine optimization techniques.

Various Terms Related To Search Engine Optimization

- White Hat SEO – Anyone who performs search engine optimization using safe and legal techniques are known as white hat SEOs. These techniques are genuine and give long lasting results. However, you do have to wait for some time before you can see results with these techniques. This technique is also known as Ethical SEO among various internet marketers.

- Black Hat SEO – This term is the one that you should be careful about. All the SEO techniques which are marked as unsafe and are not allowed by various search engines in their policies are known as Black Hat SEO techniques. These are the techniques that really attracts newbies towards them. This is because these techniques promise a quick return on the investment that you make in your online website. Unlike white hat SEO techniques, black hat SEO techniques do not give long lasting results. But there is one gift that these techniques provide to all their users, which is, getting banned. **Yes,** using these techniques gets your website banned and blacklisted in search engines. Hence, I really recommend you to stay away from all the techniques which promise you a big and quick return on your investments.

- SERP – This is the term which you will find after digging a little more on Google about SEO. SERP is the short form used for the term *Search Engine Results Page.* Do not let the big name confuse you, SERP only means the web page that a search engine displays when it is searched for a particular search term. Let's take that dog barking example again to understand that. The page that is displayed by Google when someone searches for 'how to stop a dog from barking' is known as SERP. That was easy to understand, wasn't it?

One more question in the minds of various people is how much time they need to wait for before getting results from White Hat SEO. The answer is that **it depends**. If your website has content written already and it is not optimized with SEO techniques, then it can take some time to appear in search engines with a better ranking. However, if you are just starting with your website and content then your written articles (which you will optimize for SEO purposes) will get a place in search engine pages after few months. Three months is an average time period for newbies.

Another important question that arises in the minds of newbies is can they combine the White Hat SEO techniques with Black Hat SEO techniques to get results, while fooling search engines? The answer is **NO.** Search engines are smarter than you think. Using that sort of combination will not get you banned most of the time, but will surely not improve your ranking, either.

That said, I want to tell you that you should **only use** White Hat SEO techniques for your website's SEO purposes. In the next chapter of this book, we will talk about different types of White Hat SEO techniques that you can use for your website to improve its ranking.

Various Types of White Hat SEO Techniques

Discussing all the White Hat SEO techniques is beyond the scope of this book. As I stated earlier, SEO is a big topic. Hence, I will only be discussing the techniques that are really important as per search engines requirements. In a nutshell, these techniques can be divided into two categories, namely on-page SEO techniques, and off-page SEO techniques. Let's study about them one by one.

On-Page SEO Techniques

On-Page SEO optimization is everything that you can do on your own website to make it more search engine friendly in order to increase its ranking. On-page SEO techniques constantly adapt to the web to ensure that the users receive valuable content. Hence, it is highly recommended that you keep yourself updated with latest on-page SEO techniques that are active. For example, before the hummingbird update, Google used to give high rankings in its search results to people who were writing a specific keyword in their article again and again. For example, if someone searched on Google for 'how to stop a dog from barking' then any website which used this term again and again in its article irrespective of the valuable information that it provided to the visitor used to be given a higher ranking. But, after the hummingbird update was released, Google actually started penalizing these websites by decreasing their rank, because all they wanted was traffic, and were making very few efforts to provide information to the visitor. Now, Google gives higher preference to those which are using a good website design and are providing valuable content. Based on the latest available information, below are few of the on-page SEO techniques that you can use on your website to rank it higher on Google.

Top On-Page SEO Techniques for High Ranking

Keyword Research

Keyword research is one of the best on-page SEO techniques that you can use for improving your search engine ranking. Keywords are something that a user inserts in a search engine to get results. For example, if someone searches Google for – tips for weight loss then the term – tips for weight loss is nothing but a keyword. It is always advised to write the article on your website around a certain keyword. Earlier, anyone could have gotten a high ranking on Google by repeating the keyword in their article again and again. But, this is not the case now because of the recent Google update. Still, keywords are really important to rank your website in the search engines. To be on the safe side, never overuse the same keyword again and again. Your whole article can contain a keyword density of 0.5 to 2 percent of all the words. That means if you are writing an article with keyword tips for weight loss, and your article is 1000 words, then you can use the keyword "tips for weight loss" a maximum of 20 - times and minimum 5 times.

Be Smart When Using Your Keywords

You really need to be smart when using the keyword in your article, in order to get a high ranking in Google or in any other search engine. Below are few points that you should keep in mind when using keywords your article.

- Always use the targeted keyword ONCE in the title of your article.
- Always use the targeted keyword at least once in the various headings of your article.
- Always use the targeted keyword in the first paragraph of your article.
- Always remember to insert the targeted keyword in the last paragraph of your article.
- Make sure that you always use the keyword in the URL of your article.
- You must have seen few words written below the link of the each website shown by Google in its search result. This is what we call the meta description. Each of your posts has a meta description. This is the description that search engines show in the search results. Using the

keyword in the meta description of your post is also highly recommended to get a better search engine ranking.
- You do get traffic from the default search results which depends on your article text. However, Google gives higher ranking to those articles today who also have their images optimized for SEO purposes. To optimize your images, it is highly recommended to use the targeted keyword in the alt text of your image.

Keep a Genuine Article of Proper Length

Seriously, how can you write an informative article which provides great value to your readers under 300 words? If you are trying to answer that question with a solution then I want to tell you that **you are wrong.** You can never write a proper article with informative content within 300 words. Hence, it is always recommended to keep your article length greater than 300 words. I have been blogging since 2012 and not once have I been able to write an informative blog post under 700 words. The length of your article plays an important role in your search engine ranking.

One of the misunderstandings that people have today is that writing a big article of over 1000 words will surely get you the love that you want from Google. Actually, that only happens if your article is written to provide value to your readers. Let's take an example here to understand the article length in much more detail –

Let's say that you write one article which is of 400 words length (greater than the recommended length of 300 words), and from the start to the end, it continues to provide value to your readers.

On the other hand, let's say that you wrote an article which is of 1200 words, however, it is not as informative as your 400-word article. Most of the words in the article are used to tell stories which are not providing any value to your readers.

In this case, Google will give more preference in search rankings to the 400 word article, rather than giving a higher rank to the 1200 word article.

Hence, always remember to write valuable content on your website while keeping the word length greater than 300.

Provide a Great User Experience to Your Readers

The recent Google update changed everything, now, you must use keywords in a smart manner, and must provide a great user experience to your readers. Your website is said to provide a rich user experience if it follows the points mentioned below –

- Your website should not have tons of ads running on it.
- Your website should have an easy navigation system to help your readers surfing on your website.
- Your website should provide ease of access to all your posts and pages to your readers.
- You should take care to use the proper font on your website. Your website may get penalized for using a font that is not easy to read. Moreover, if you are using a proper font, then you should take care of the font size as well. Remember that the font size will also decide how user-friendly your website really is. Do not use so small font size that your users actually start to strain their eyes while trying to read. Neither should you use too big a font size.
- Besides using the proper font and the font size, you should also provide a good reading experience to your readers. No one likes to read big paragraphs today, they turn out to be boring rather than engaging. Hence, to provide

a good reading experience to your readers, I recommend you to use small paragraphs of three to four lines in order to keep your article well formatted for reading purposes.

- Most people today use different kind of devices to read, some use their laptop, while others use their tablets and then there are people like me who do most of their internet surfing and reading activities on their smartphones. Hence, you should use a flexible design for your website in order to increase your search engine rankings. You need to make sure that your website is responsive in design. A website's design is said to be responsive if it adjusts itself according to the screen size to provide a better reading experience along with ease of access to your readers.

Remember Content Is the King

Okay, so let's say that you are using all the tips for on-page SEO that I have mentioned until now in this book. But still, chances are that you are not seeing good improvements in your search ranking on

Google and other search engines. This is because your content is not up to the mark. What I mean here is that the content that you have written either has grammatical mistakes or is already available on the internet.

You can correct the grammatical mistakes, but being already available is something that you need to pay attention to. You can rewrite an article to pass the plagiarism check. But, Google is smart enough to point out that all the content that you have written has already been sitting on the internet for quite some time. Hence, you should always write an original article. If the idea of your article is already taken by others, then you should find a unique niche in that article to make it rank higher in search engines.

Let's examine an example to understand this better. Let's say that you want to write an article on weight loss for women, but there are several articles on that topic already. So, to add the unique niche, you can write the article as – weight loss for women during pregnancy. I hope you have an idea of where to find a unique niche now. Remember, no matter how good your SEO techniques are, content is the undefeated king which is given highest priority by search engines. Thus, you should always write an article that is –

- Free from plagiarism and grammatical mistakes
- Has a unique niche if required
- Should provide value to the readers

Page Load Speed

This is another important point in On-Page SEO techniques. You should design your website in such a way that it takes less time to load a page. How will a person read when your website takes ages to load the page? He will end up getting irritated and will eventually hit the back button to find some other website on search results. The more time your website takes to load itself, the less love you will receive from Google in your search ranking. Your website's page load speed plays an important role in the user experience.

Never Ignore the Internal Links

Using internal links is often ignored by beginners. They really do not know how important internal links are for SEO purposes. Keeping that in mind, I will be explaining the concept of internal links to you in detail.

So, what is interlinking or internal links? Basically, internal links are the links on a page of a particular website, which lead to another page or post on the same website. A perfect example of an internal link is Related Posts. The section of related posts has links to other articles.

These links can be to anywhere on the same website. They can be to the home page of the website, or to the privacy page, or to any other article or blog post.

Okay, so, that being said, now let's move on to another important question related to internal links —

Why Are Internal Links So Important?

Many people today see internal links as a method to make the connection between their posts. However, the search engines do not see internal links in the same manner. In the eyes of search engines like Bing, Yahoo, Google, etc., internal links are a method to notify users of the **important content** on the other pages of the same website. Other reasons of internal links being important are –

- They tell your readers about other posts available on your website, which are relevant to the current post that they are reading. Thus, giving you points in providing better navigation, reading experiences and rich user experiences, which ultimately boosts your SEO rank.
- When you link internally, you have a great chance to target a particular keyword. Most people who create related posts **manually** for their website today practice this technique to increase their SEO rank. I made the word 'manually' bold because most of the people who are running their websites on platforms like WordPress use plugins for creating related posts automatically. These plugins mainly target posts from the same category, rather than targeting a particular keyword.
- Using internal links is an excellent method to help search engines to crawl your website more efficiently. The better they crawl, the more

links they will find and better your SEO ranking will be for several keywords.

So, did you see how important internal links are for SEO purposes? Next time, think twice before ignoring them.

Say NO to content barriers

By content barriers, I mean pop-ups, overlays, and interstitials. Google really hates websites which use these means to cover the content as soon as the reader lands on their website. I have written about each of these in detail in the points below –

- You may be using pop-ups on your website to get social likes or for getting subscribers to your email list. However, if you do the same while hiding the main content from the user, then Google may penalize you.
- You may be thinking that you can use interesting overlays to promote your other articles or to promote some of your events or products. While you are correct, overdoing the same will lower your SEO rank.

- Using interstitials is great, even top websites like Forbes do it. However, they have strong SEO behind their work and just using interstitials won't harm their SEO ranking. Moreover, they are not using interstitials when the reader is reading the content, they show them the interstitial when he is about to land on their website. If you are going to use interstitials to show ads or for any sort of promotion when the user is reading on your website, then you are making a big mistake in the eyes of Google and other search engines.

Be Professional – Have All the Required Pages

This is one of the biggest mistakes which newbies commit towards SEO. Google and any other search engine give appropriate attention to the pages that you have on your website. They see that you have all the relevant pages on your website before crediting you with SEO points for them. These relevant pages are –

- About Page
- Disclaimer Page
- Terms Of Service Page
- Privacy Policy Page
- Contact Page

Out the pages that I have mentioned above, you cannot miss even one as doing so will affect your SEO ranking in the eyes of search engines.

Some of the top advertisers like Bing Ads and Google Adwords never accept a website for advertising purposes if they do not have the pages that I have mentioned above. Even if you are paying them for advertisement, they still do not compromise with their policies and quality of their service. So, how can you expect them to be ignorant on the same subject for giving a SEO ranking?

Hence, no matter what, you should have these pages on your website. If you are just starting with your website, then I highly recommend you to get these pages even before you start posting the content there.

So, that was it with the On-page SEO techniques. It was quite a list, wasn't it? If you will follow all the advice that I provided in this chapter and you are good to go. Now, let's start with the Off-page SEO techniques and see what you can do there to improve your search engine rankings.

Off-page SEO Techniques

So, let's begin by first understanding what off-page SEO really is.

On-page SEO optimization is everything that you do on your website to improve its overall ranking in search engines like Google, Yahoo, Bing, etc.

Beginners never make it to on-page SEO optimization (but you will as I have provided you with the techniques for the same in this chapter), and some of the smart beginners or intermediates who make it to on-page SEO optimization start to think that it is the end of their SEO hustle. However, I just want to remind you what I said at the start –

SEO is a big and complex task.

Once you are done with implementing the On-page SEO, it is time to start with Off-page SEO optimization. **Why?** Because various other things which are important in the eyes of Google happen outside your website. Depending on the goals that you have in mind for your website or blog, your time doing Off-page SEO optimization will vary.

However, just like On-page SEO optimization, beginners can be overwhelmed with Off-page SEO optimization as well. Because the tasks that you can perform off-page to boost your SEO rankings are huge.

Just like On-page SEO Optimization, I will discuss various Off-page SEO techniques with you that you can use for impressing Google. I want you to remember that Off-page SEO is nothing but a way to tell Google what others on the internet think of your website. If you have quality backlinks from others to your website, then this will indicate to Google that you have great content, otherwise, why would people spend time linking back to your website?

Off-page SEO Techniques for Impressing Google

Okay, so let's start discussing the relevant techniques. All the techniques that I will mention here are tested and can be applied by beginners with no problems.

Never Underestimate Article Directories

Most people think that off-page SEO is only about building backlinks to your website by commenting on other people's blogs or websites. This is not totally true and there are other ways as well. One of them being article directories. I must say that this is one of the most underrated methods and yet it is very powerful to get you some quality backlinks.

In the article directory method, you submit some of your original articles to various article directories available on the internet. These articles contain a backlink to your website hence helping you to get a quality backlink. Below is an example to tell you how you can do the same for your website.

Let's say that your website has an article on juicing recipes for weight loss. What you can now do is make an original article explaining what juices can help in weight loss and can submit that article to an article directory while including a link at the end to the juice recipes for weight loss. Similarly, you can create many original articles linked to the same main article and submit them to other article directories to get a backlink from them.

Do Guest Blogging Often

Writing on your own main website is required, but you should definitely write on other people's websites as well.

The process of writing an article on another website which is in the same niche as your original website is known as guest blogging.

Guest blogging is a great method to make some back links from websites of the same niche as this will boost your SEO ranking massively. Why? Because Google understands that if a website in the same niche as your main website is giving you a backlink, then you must have some great content on your website.

To do a guest blog post, you can contact the admins of other websites via their contact page and ask them for permissions for the same. You will surely see a big improvement in your SEO ranking soon once you do guest blogging.

Let's Understand the Commenting System

I said earlier in this section that Off-page SEO is not only about commenting. But, if you do want to make some backlinks via commenting then do it the right way.

Make backlinks to your website by making **genuine** comments on the other niche related websites. For example, if your website is in the skin care niche, then you should try to get a back link to your website by making a **genuine** comment on some other website which is in the skin care niche as well.

I wrote the word 'genuine' in bold. Why? Because I want you to know that making genuine comments is really necessary. This is because most of the website admins have comment moderation turned ON. Thus, they can see the comment that you made even before it is visible to others including search engines. If they find out that your comment is not related to the respective post, then they will delete your comment right away.

Another good practice to get backlinks via commenting is to comment on various niche-related forum posts. It is easier to get your comments approved in forums that is on personal or branded niche-related websites.

Besides posting comments to the forums, you can also be an active member there and can get backlinks by writing about your main website in your forum posts or in your signature in your forum profile.

Do Not Forget Social Sharing

You must have seen 'sharing is caring' written on various websites. And that is true as well. Not only for websites but also for Off-page SEO purposes. Sharing your content on the social platforms helps you in earning more and more backlinks from them, thus improving your off-page SEO optimization.

One question that I am always asked when I am talking about Social shares and SEO is do search engines use social data to improve SEO rankings?

The answer to that question is NO, they do not. Although every social engine has its power crawling algorithm, but they have their limits as well. They can never crawl all the links and when it comes to social media, they cannot even crawl most of the links, in order to prevent themselves from getting blocked by those social sites.

Remember that social sharing will work differently to help you in your SEO ranking. They will not directly help search engines but they will drive organic traffic to your website which every search engine can see. The more traffic you will have, the more that page will be crawled by search engines and the higher its ranking will be in their search results for the targeted keywords.

In a nutshell, using social sites and doing social sharing helps you with your SEO indirectly.

So that was it with the social sharing and Off-page SEO techniques. In the next chapter, I will tell you about content marketing and social media marketing.

Content Marketing & Social Media Marketing

Most of the time I talk about creating and sharing content on the web, people term it either as content marketing or as social media marketing. More than 90% of people I talk to are always confused about these two topics. While they may seem to be one and the same thing, there is a huge difference between them. Both of them are an integral part of internet marketing (also known as online marketing by some people). To make your business a success, you need to pay attention to both content marketing and social media marketing. However, this seems to be impossible for newbies as they do not know the difference between the two. At the end of this post, I want you to remember that both of these marketing strategies are used solely for promoting your website or business in the online market. In this chapter, I will explain to you what Content Marketing and Social Media marketing are. This will also help you in understanding the difference between the two as well. So, let's start with Content Marketing.

Content Marketing

Content Marketing is the process of creating content for your audience. All the work done under content marketing is usually in the form of blog posts or articles on the website. The type of content that you create on your website depends on the type of your business.

For example, if your business is nothing but a blog about skin care products, then your articles will be blog posts reviewing or promoting those skin care products and nothing else. Similarly, if your business is about your own skin care products, then your articles will be a review of your own skin care products along with the sales letter for your audience to view the product purchasing page.

One thing that you need to keep in mind when creating the content for your website is that it needs to be of high quality.

So, what does high-quality content looks like? Content is said to be of high quality if it delivers what the user wants. You will better understand it with an example –

Let's say that you have a blog post titled as "Weight Loss Tips for Pregnancy". But if the content in the article body is just general weight loss tips for general fitness, then the content is not what your article title promises to deliver. Anyone who reads this article after reading the title will surely be disappointed. This type of content is known as bad quality content. Similarly, if your article body provides exactly what you promised in your article title, then the user will not only read your content but will also share it with others. This kind of content, which delivers what is promised, is known as high quality or good quality content. Other important points worth mentioning about good content are –

- It is optimized for SEO purposes.
- It is free from any sort of plagiarism and grammatical mistakes.

- It is well formatted.
- It discusses the topic in detail.
- It is easy to share with others.

Now that you know what content marketing is and why you should have high-quality content for your marketing purposes. Let's learn about the importance of using content marketing –

- It's a great way to engage people on your website, who can later be turned into customers.
- It increases the chances of success for your business when you combine it with social media marketing.
- Content marketing helps in improving the SEO ranking of your website.

Now, let's move on to social media marketing and see how it is different from content marketing.

Social Media Marketing

Social media marketing acts as a supplement to content marketing. In content marketing, the focus is on the content that you write, you must make sure that it is of high quality to **engage** the readers. On the other hand, in social media marketing, you promote your business on several social media platforms like Twitter, Facebook, etc. by writing content which makes your followers **participate.**

Content marketing is totally about adding information while social media marketing is about increasing people's participation. Besides, the type of content on social media marketing includes images, quotes, videos, gifs, and other animations which are relevant to your business. Today, social media marketing is used by all the leading bloggers, webmasters, and business owners to increase their fan's participation.

In content marketing, we engage them with our content to turn them into our customers. In social media marketing, we make the people participate in various activities, and, in turn, earn revenue from them later. These activities can be –

- Asking questions, so that you can know what article to write next in your content marketing.

- Running surveys, so that you can know what problems they are actually suffering from, so as you can recommend them the products for the same.
- Posting infographics which can be used to increase their participation in a particular area, that later can be analyzed for both content marketing ideas and for product recommendation ideas.

So, do you see how social media marketing can help you with your business? Besides the benefits I mentioned above, social media marketing also helps in —

- Increasing the brand awareness among people.
- Building a loyal and active fan following.
- Finding new and potential customers.
- Staying one step ahead of your competitors.

Can you make a difference with just one type of marketing?

This is another question that people ask me, often as soon as they understand the difference between social media marketing and content marketing. And the answer is both yes and no. **Yes** because something is always better than nothing. Using any one of these two marketing techniques will surely improve your business performance. **No,** because if you do not combine both marketing techniques, then after some time, you will notice that the performance vs time graph of your business is a straight line being parallel to the time axis. Meaning, you will not notice many improvements with time. Hence, it is highly recommended that you use both of these marketing skills in your business to make it the success that you always wanted.

Continuing our talk on the search engine optimization, you must have noticed that I have mentioned one of the terms several times in this book, that is, **keywords.** In the next chapter of this book, I will tell you about the various uses of keywords and how to find keywords for the same.

Everything that you need to know about Keywords

Okay, so I have already provided you with a general introduction to keywords, which explain what keywords are. If you do not know what I am talking about, then I highly recommend you to read the On-page SEO section again.

Continuing our discussion on keywords, let's understand more about their importance and uses.

Importance of Using Keywords & Keyword Research

- Using keywords tells search engines what your article is about. Similarly, they also tell them what your website is about. If you want to rank in search engines then you should not use keywords in your articles which are blacklisted by them. A few examples of these keywords are – crack, hack, jail break, mod, etc.

- Doing keyword research is an excellent way to find new ideas for creating content for your website.
- Keyword research also helps you in finding various low competition keywords for your business. These keywords, when used in your articles, have a reader appeal for over two years of time. Meaning, the content that you will create with these keywords will remain SEO optimized for at least 2 years of time. That is why these keywords are also referred to as gold keywords by some marketers.
- A proper keyword research reveals various ideas that you can use for creating a new business as well.
- A proper keyword research also helps in writing detailed sales letters for your products which increases the chances of conversion of your reader into your customer.

I'm sure that I've got your attentions for keywords. The very next question that beginners have always asked me out of excitement after learning these benefits is – Where can I find these keywords? The answer is to use various keyword research tools –

Keyword Research Tools for Finding New Keywords

Keyword research tools are programs which help you by providing you the niche-specific keyword on the basis of a seed keyword that you provide to them.

Let's take an example to understand what seed keyword and niche specific keywords are –

Let's say that you want to write an article for your website for weight loss. Then what you will do is that you will write 'weight loss' in the keyword research tool. The tool will then give you a lot of keywords which are all related to weight loss, like weight loss for adults.

In this example above, the term that you provided to the tool, namely weight loss, is the seed keyword. A keyword that the tool used to start its research. And the various keywords that it provided to you based on the seed keyword are known as the niche specific keywords (like weight loss for adults).

You should always do a detailed research in a similar manner to generate various keyword ideas for your business. For now, let's stick to our discussion and learn about various keyword research tools that you can use for this purpose.

Google Keyword Planner Tool

This is a free keyword planner tool that is provided by Google to all its AdWords users.

Another misunderstanding the beginners have in their mind is that they actually need to pay for Google Adwords in order to use it. However, the reality is totally different. Inside Google AdWords, you need to pay **only** for the ads that you will create using their keyword planner tool. The keyword research that you can do with this tool is always free for everyone.

To access the keyword planner tool, log in to your AdWords account (if you do not have one, then create one using your existing Google account). Then go to tools and click keyword planner.

Once you are inside the keyword planner, you will see something that reads 'Find new keywords and get search volume data' and under that you will see an option to search for new keywords using phrases, click on it. Do not worry as keyword phrases are the seed keywords.

Now, the tool will provide you with what I call the keyword research form. Fill it as per the directions below –

- Write your seed keyword in the tab that says – your product or service.
- Leave the landing page tab blank.
- Select your product category to find the specific keywords. However, I generally leave this tab blank so that I can see all the potential keywords for my niche.
- In the Targeting section, you can select the country that you want to target your audience from.
- In the "customize your search section," you can add more keywords, or filter some keywords

out of your research according to their searches, etc.

After filling out this keyword research form, simply click to get several keyword ideas from Google. Now, once Google is done with generating ideas, it will show you the result in two tabs –

- Ad group ideas – These are the keyword ideas that are being used by advertisers for creating their ad on Google. We are not interested in these right now.
- Keyword Ideas – This section contains various keywords that people are actually inserting in Google to find the websites and articles that they can get value from. This is the section that is worth spending time on. From this section, you can find various keywords that you can use for your business. Target the keywords with low competition from the keywords list and use them to improve your business and SEO ranking.

Long Tail Keyword Pro

This is a desktop application and is a more simplified form of the keyword research tool. This tool was created after seeing the complexity in finding the low competition keywords from Google Adwords. Unlike Google's keyword planner tool, Long Tail Keyword Pro comes with a price. Long Tail Keyword Pro helps you in finding keywords with low competition that you can use for your business. The twist is that for every keyword idea that it generates for you, it provides you with the keyword's competitiveness. This keyword competitiveness is the measure of how low the competition is for that particular keyword. If the value for the keyword competitiveness for a particular keyword is less than 35 then it is marked as safe and recommended for use in content marketing.

Jaaxy

Jaaxy is another keyword research tool which comes at a price. However, the advantage of Jaaxy over Long Tail Keyword Pro is that it is simpler to use, and is faster in compiling keyword ideas for you. Another point worth mentioning here is that Jaaxy generates keyword ideas for finding low competition keywords by gathering data from Bing, Yahoo, and Google. Long Tail Keyword Pro on the other hand only gathers the data from Google. Hence, when you are using Jaaxy for your keyword research, you are targeting more than one search engine thus improving your SEO to a large extent. The recommendation of Jaaxy for finding keyword ideas is that it generates very simple ones. If Jaaxy shows a green light with a keyword, then it means that you can use that particular keyword in your business. If it shows a yellow light, then it means that it is your call for that keyword as the level of competition for that particular keyword is moderate. If the red light is shown by jaaxy, well, we all know that red is the color of danger, don't we?

SEMrush

This is another paid keyword research tool. Along with helping you in finding various keywords for your business, SEMrush also offers an option to spy on your competitors. All you have to do is enter a URL for a particular article from your competitor's website and SEMrush will show you all the keywords that your competitor is using to rank his business in various search engines. This keyword list can then be used for your business to create new articles or to rank for the same keywords (if they are of low competition) in your existing articles.

Keyword.io

This is another free yet powerful keyword research tool. It is also known as the best alternative for the Google AdWords' keyword planner tool. When you are using this tool, you can set the Google domain that you want to use for your keyword research. For example, if you are planning to target audiences from the USA for your business, then you can select Google.com as your Google domain. Similarly, if you are planning to target audience from the UK for your business, then you can select Google.co.uk as your Google domain. The tool will then do its research and will present you with keywords that are both niche-specific and geographical area specific. Of course you can do the same with Google Adwords but a simple process does help in your keyword research.

My Personal Recommendation

I have used all the tools that I have mentioned in this chapter and my personal recommendation for you is to either go with Long Tail Keyword Pro or with SEMrush. I know they are paid tools, but once you use them, you will realize that they are worth every penny spent. These two tools have really helped me in boosting my business and its search engine ranking.

In the next chapter, I will tell you why advertising your business is important and how you can do the same with the help of Google Adwords.

Marketing with Google Adwords

I have told you about the various types of SEO techniques and two main marketing techniques that you can use for making your business a success. However, an important part of online marketing is marketing your business itself. More and more people will learn about your business if you advertise it on leading search engines like Google.

Why is it important to advertise your business?

- The primary objective of advertising your business is promotion. You will promote your business to the world with the help of Google Adwords. The more promotion you do, the more people will learn about you and more chances of your business getting established by building a large audience.
- Another objective of advertising your business is to spread awareness among people. Surely you started a business to fill a hole in the marketing or industry that has been sitting

there for quite a while. If there was no such hole then you would not have started this business. Because there will not be any profit and anything without profit is not a business, it's charity.

- According to Gerard Tellis, the person behind *"Effective Advertising: Understanding When, How, and Why Advertising Works"*, advertising helps people compare you with your competitors. The more comparisons they do, the better they'll understand why you'll provide them more value than your competitors.

Advertising has always been an integral part of any business, both offline and online. This section must have helped you in understanding how important the online advertising is today.

Now, let's move further and learn how you can set up an ad that will help your business make a profit.

How to set up a profitable ad using Google Adwords

Okay, so since this book was written keeping beginners in mind, I will be explaining this method from scratch, so that even a newbie who just started their online journey can benefit from it.

Starting a fresh ad campaign on Google Adwords can be really overwhelming and most people. Even some experienced internet marketers commit mistakes because of all the fear, tension and excitement that their mind is absorbing in their fight to just finish the process and to click the Start Campaign button.

I remember my first ad campaign on Google, which I created within a few minutes and felt happy about, thinking that I had started an ad and now would get a lot of revenue out of it. The result, however, was the opposite. Forget the revenue, my ad did not even find me an audience.

- Start by signing in to your Google Adwords Account. Now, click on tool and then select

keyword planner. Now, select 'search for new keywords using a phrase...' section to open the keyword planner form.
- The first step of starting a profitable ad using Google AdWords is understanding your audience type. Are you targeting people who want to read, or are you targeting people who want to buy? Accordingly, you have to use the Google AdWords' keyword planner tool. Words like "best, top, etc." are often used to target people who want to buy something online. If you are not looking for them, then you should apply a filter for these words when you are filling out the keyword planner form to find new keyword ideas for your business. You can enter these words in the 'negative keywords' section to exclude the keywords which contain them.
- Before you hit the get ideas button, make sure that you have set the correct geographical location for your audience. Setting this option

is highly recommended to make an amazing ad in Google AdWords.

- Once you generate ideas for your business, you will see two tabs, one is the keyword idea, and another is the ad group idea. This time, you will need to stick to the ad group ideas.

Once you see various keywords ideas, you will see the following tabs related to their data –

- Average Monthly Searches – This column will explain to you about how many searches are being made for that particular keyword from the people of the geographical location that you set.
- Competition – This will tell you how much competition is going on in AdWords among the advertisers to get their ad places for that particular keyword.
- Suggested Bid – This will show you the amount of money that advertising is paying. This is calculated by keeping average Cost per Click in mind.

- Ignore all the other columns as we do not need them for setting up your ad right now, they are just a distraction.

Now, it's time to ask yourself few questions, these questions will help you in selecting a keyword that will generate you profit without making a hole in your pocket. So, let's start –

- Ask yourself; is the keyword okay for your business intent? Meaning is the keyword shown to you good for finding potential buyers or not (if you are launching ad to find people who buy products online). Look out for the buying words that I told you about before in this chapter.
- Next, you should ask yourself; does this keyword have a search volume in Google? If no, then why would you select a keyword and pay for it when people are not even looking for it on the internet? Select only a keyword which has at least 2000 average monthly searches for it on the internet.

- The number of search results shown to you by Google on an average basis is not always accurate. For example, if you try to post an ad for Christmas during December, then the monthly searches for the keywords related to Christmas will be at their maximum in December, and the search results will not be the same for January. Hence, after filtering your keywords based on the average monthly searches, you should filter them again on their trend. You can see the Google trends graph for every keyword by clicking the small graph icon that is available in its average monthly searches column.
- Once you are done with the Google trends, it is now time to move on and decide which keywords to keep based on their competition and suggested bid. Always remember that higher competition and higher suggested big means that your chances of targeting traffic with that keyword and turning that traffic into audience or customers is comparatively higher

than the keywords which have lower suggested big and low competition. AD setup works differently than the keywords ideas tab. In the keyword ideas tab, we look for keywords with low competition to create content, while in setting up a profitable ad, we go with the keyword with high competition to make our business a success. Always remember the difference between the two.
- Now, if you have followed the directions correctly, you have comparatively fewer keywords than what Google Adwords showed you. Now, it is time to ask yourself the most important question, **which of these keywords can you afford with your budget.** You certainly will not want to target the keywords which are not in your budget. It is a golden rule of advertising that you should advertise for only the amount that you can stand up for without going into debt. Hence, out of the keywords that you have selected following the process till now, you should now select a final list of keywords based on your budget.

To decide your budget, you can use the review plan tab from Google Adwords' keyword planner tool research results. Below is the process to do calculate your budget with your selected keywords –

- Once you have selected the keywords and are ready to filter them out based on your budget, download those keywords on your computer from the download button provided on the right side of the keyword and ad group idea tabs. Now, from the top of your screen, you will see the **Find Keywords** tab being set as active. Just after that tab, you will see **Review Plan** tab, click on this tab.
- Now, it will say that you do not have any keywords in your plan and will provide you an option to upload the keywords. Just upload the file of filtered keywords that you downloaded from the ad group ideas tab.
- Once you are done with uploading the file, the review plan tab will provide you with a graph which shows the daily estimate for your selected keywords for activities like

impressions, clicks, and will also provide you with a graph of cost per click.
- Above that graph, you will see a performance forecast text written where you can enter your daily bid. In this section, you need to enter the daily CPC (cost per click) bid that you are willing to pay for the keywords that you have selected.
- Once you provide the bid, the table of your keywords that can be found below the graph will refresh and will show you the estimate for daily traffic and daily cost for the keywords.
- At the end of the table, you will see a row named **Total,** this row will tell you the total daily estimate for your keywords.
- To decide your budget on monthly basis, all you have to do is to multiply the value of cost for a total estimate with 30.4 (the average of a number of days in a month).
- The value that you will get is your expenses for a month of advertising with Google Adwords. If the expense is affordable to you, then congrats, you have successfully found all the profitable

keywords that you can use to create your ad. If not then it is time to reconsider your keywords.
- From your selected keywords, start removing keywords on a stricter basis of the search term and suggested bid. It is all trial and error. Doing this will help you find all the keywords that you can use to create a monthly ad campaign which is within your budget.

So that was it with setting up a profitable ad for your business using Google AdWords. One thing to remember is that AdWords is really powerful but still your total budget may vary as the amount that AdWords shows for suggested bid is not always accurate. Hence, it is always recommended to use the review plan method that I have provided above to select the keywords according to your budget.

Conclusion

I hope that you have enjoyed this book. One thing that I want to tell you is that SEO is not something that you can set and forget. It is not a technique that will continue to work for you if your website is alive on the internet.

You need to understand that SEO is an ongoing process, it never ends. The more improvements you can do, the better. Before you can reach a point in your improvements where you can say that you are done with your SEO, you will find out that Google has changed its search engine optimization ranking to provide more valuable content to its users. You can never expect an SEO algorithm to be constant, it always changes and to deliver quality content, it will keep changing in the future as well.

Finally, I want to congratulate you for completing your SEO study. Now, it is time for you to take action because this book is of no use if you only read it, write a word about it on the internet and then forget it. To actually get value out of this book, you will have to apply it to your business or blog. The more time you spend in applying the techniques in this book, the better you will become in your SEO research and ranking techniques.

www.ingramcontent.com/pod-product-compliance
Lightning Source LLC
Chambersburg PA
CBHW072108290426
44110CB00014B/1864